A WINDOW ON WILLIAMSBURG

A Window on Williamsburg

Photographs by TAYLOR LEWIS, JR.

Text by JOHN J. WALKLET, JR.
and THOMAS K. FORD

THE COLONIAL WILLIAMSBURG FOUNDATION
Williamsburg, Virginia

Distributed by HOLT, RINEHART AND WINSTON, NEW YORK, NEW YORK

B RIGHT as the gold that lured adventurers to the New World, a
dandelion thrusts its shaggy head above the gnarled roots of a
Williamsburg tree. Just as it flowered in this unlikely spot, so the seed
of English settlement planted at Jamestown blossomed on the edge of the
wilderness. Transplanted to Williamsburg after nearly a century, the seedling
of empire flourished here.

Williamsburg was one of the most important training grounds for the
leaders of American independence. For eighty-one years (1699-1780) it was
Virginia's colonial and state capital, a political and cultural center that ranked
in importance with Boston, Philadelphia, Newport, Charleston, Annapolis,
and New York. Here George Washington, Patrick Henry, George Wythe,
Thomas Jefferson, George Mason, and other patriots helped to shape the
foundations of our government.

The prosperous little city those great men knew is the one we see today,
restored to its appearance of the years before and during the Revolution. The
preservation project, inspired by Dr. W. A. R. Goodwin and launched in 1926
with the guidance and support of John D. Rockefeller, Jr., continues under
the supervision of the Colonial Williamsburg Foundation, a publicly
supported foundation.

Next two pages: the Palace fish pond or
"canal" with its chinoiserie footbridge.

A little girl's garden needs a fence . . .   for little birds to perch upon

    . . . for silken cats to slip under   . . . and hollyhocks to gossip over.

The
brilliant
disarray
of autumn
blurs some
lines . . .

. . . while
it sharpens
others in
the garden
geometry of
Williamsburg.

Catalpa trees along the Palace Green, seedpods dangling from their
newly barren branches, frame a latticework view of autumn's fading colors.

THE CAPITOL

*"What a temptation to sit in silence and let the past speak
to us of those great patriots whose voices once
resounded in these halls, and whose farseeing wisdom,
high courage, and unselfish devotion to the common
good will ever be an inspiration to noble living."*

—JOHN D. ROCKEFELLER, JR.

To attentive ears the echoes of stirring events still resound in the Hall of the House of Burgesses. This was the scene of Patrick Henry's "Caesar-Brutus" speech and his defiant resolutions opposing the Stamp Act; of George Mason's Virginia Declaration of Rights; the May 15, 1776, Resolution for Independence, which led directly to Philadelphia and the July 4 Declaration; the pioneering Virginia constitution of that same year, model for many other states; and the introduction of Thomas Jefferson's famous Statute for Religious Freedom.

Contrasting with the austerity of the Hall of the House of Burgesses, luxury characterizes the Council Chamber. The upper house of colonial Virginia's legislature, the Council was an appointive body. Members selected from among the colony's landed aristocracy served at the behest of the crown. Quite a few, nevertheless—like the Nelsons of Yorktown and John Page of Rosewell—ardently supported independence and paid dearly for it.

The General Court, highest judicial tribunal in the colony, met twice yearly here in the Capitol. Civil cases occupied most of its attention, but criminal offenses punishable by mutilation or death also came before it. In this setting the fifteen survivors of Blackbeard's pirate crew faced trial, thirteen of them being sentenced to hang for their crimes.

Framed by massive candlesticks, portraits of Edmund Pendleton, John Robinson, and Patrick Henry—each a power in the political life of Virginia—lend dignity to the Conference Room of the Capitol. Here councilors and burgesses met to conduct morning prayer and to resolve legislative differences between their two houses.

THE
GOVERNOR'S
PALACE

A likeness of Elizabeth I, painted by
Marcus Geerarts the Elder about
1585, dominates the Secretary's
office in the Capitol.

"George Washington at the Battle of
Trenton," by Charles Willson Peale,
hangs in the hallway of the Capitol.
The general was forty-five years old
at the time.

ERECTED to provide an appropriate residence for the king's deputy, the "Palace" promptly acquired its name—originally a derisive one—from unhappy taxpayers. It housed seven royal governors, from Alexander Spotswood, the soldier architect who supervised its construction, to the tactless John Murray, earl of Dunmore, whose flight to the safety of a warship in the York River ended British rule in Virginia. The Palace also served as the executive mansion for Patrick Henry and Thomas Jefferson, the first and second elected governors of the commonwealth of Virginia.

A commanding portrait of Governor Spotswood watches over the intimate family dining room *(opposite page)*. The rare silver chandelier, made in the 1690s by England's Daniel Garnier, once graced the royal St. James's Palace in London.

The governor's office, in the East Advance Building, is distinctly a man's room. Its functional furnishings were selected with an eye to the comfort and convenience of the king's appointees.

The state dining room, where the governor and his lady might entertain their guests. A double-pagoda silver epergne fashioned about 1762 by Thomas Pitts, an English silversmith, decorates the elegant mahogany table, which was made about the same time. Chelsea porcelain figurines, such as those listed in the 1770 Palace inventory after the death of Lord Botetourt, line the mantel. Above it hangs a portrait of King James I of England by the Italian painter, Fredrigo Zuccaro.

Opposite page: Acoustically superb and elegant in decor, the Palace ballroom again resounds on appropriate occasions with sprightly airs of colonial days. Jacob Kirckman of London made the double-keyboard harpsichord in 1762.

The artistry of master cabinetmakers is evident in the parlor. John Wentworth, last royal governor of New Hampshire, once owned the "Chinese Chippendale" settee and armchair.

A silver monteith on the center table and a crystal chandelier above it reflect the light from every window of the supper room. Guests who had danced and supped could step out for a garden stroll.

Summer heat calls for gauze curtains on the bed in the spacious northeast bedchamber. A silver urn or "tea kitchen" of Sheffield plate presides over the breakfast table.

Sitting before the mirror of the shaving stand in his bedchamber, His Excellency's twentieth-century self adjusts his wig.

A chair for the gentleman suffering from gout—the footrest rises as the back tilts down—joins other sickroom articles temporarily arranged in the southwest bedchamber.

Opposite page:
A scatter of books and paper in the second-floor sitting room at the Palace suggests that the governor finds it a convenient place to work at night. Spanish leather covering the walls corresponds to the "gilt leather hangings" specified in a 1710 "Proposal For rendering the new House Convenient as well as Ornamental."

Opposite page:

BRUTON PARISH CHURCH

Bruton Parish was formed in 1674 by the merger of two earlier parishes. The present church, designed by Governor Spotswood, was completed in 1715 and a tower was added in 1769. It has been in continuous use since the days when church and state were united in Virginia and this edifice represented the established Anglican authority in the colony.

THE COURTHOUSE OF 1770

On July 26, 1776, the Declaration of Independence was proclaimed to the people of Williamsburg from the steps of this building. It has stood here on Market Square for two centuries, housing—until 1932—both the municipal court of Williamsburg and the county court of James City County. The latter in colonial times was the principal agent of local government in Virginia, exercising executive as well as judicial powers.

THE WREN BUILDING

The oldest academic building in English America, with its varying roof lines,
massive chimneys, and lofty cupola, the Wren Building dominates the
College of William and Mary yard. Its foundation was laid in 1695.

Here in the Common Room the professors could relax, and valuable "philosophic" apparatus could be kept safely out of student reach.

The master of the Grammar School and his chief usher prepared boys of twelve to sixteen for college. They taught Latin, Greek, mathematics, and penmanship, and their discipline was strict.

THE POWDER MAGAZINE
and GUARDHOUSE

The Magazine, built in 1715, held the colony's military equipment and gunpowder. As tempers rose in 1775, Governor Dunmore thought it prudent to remove the powder from patriot reach. His surreptitious attempt was discovered—and that spark ignited the tinder of Revolution in Virginia.

THE PUBLIC GAOL

Petty miscreants could suffer tortured hours in the pillory *(left)* or the stocks, while debtors and common criminals might languish for months inside this "strong, sweet Prison." Completed in 1704, even before the Capitol, the gaol remained in constant use, sometimes as a military prison and later as the city jail of Williamsburg, until 1910.

HOMES and GARDENS

In accord with the city's basic law, Williamsburg building lots were
capacious: half an acre each. The law also required that they be fenced.

JAMES GEDDY HOUSE
FOUNDRY and SILVERSMITH SHOP

James Geddy and his sons were craftsmen and solid citizens. James the elder, gunsmith and brass founder, built the main part of the house in the 1750s. His sons David and William took over when he died, offering their services in the "Gun-Smith's, Cutler's, and Founder's Trades." Apparently they did blacksmithing and farriery, too. James the younger became one of the town's foremost silversmiths. Extensive archaeological excavation of the property has turned up artifacts from all these trades.

The younger James Geddy also repaired clocks and watches, and for a time his brother-in-law, William Waddill, joined him here as silversmith and engraver.

Opposite page: Molten metal never fails to provide a spectacular display of sparks and fumes in the Geddy foundry.

In the front bedroom of the Geddy
House cluttered writing materials
and toilet articles on the desk
emphasize that any room in a small
colonial home might have to serve
several functions.

The furnishings of the
Geddy hall reflect
Mr. Geddy's
economic and social
status as probably the
foremost practitioner
of his craft in
Williamsburg and a
respected member of
the city's Common
Council.

GEORGE WYTHE HOUSE

This was the home of a distinguished Virginian whose public career spanned a decisive half-century in American life. One of the foremost classical scholars in the colonies, George Wythe befriended a young student at the College of William and Mary, Thomas Jefferson, who later studied law in Wythe's office and referred to him as "my faithful and beloved Mentor in youth, and my most affectionate friend through life." John Marshall, too, studied under him. Wythe was executor and close friend of royal governors Fauquier and Botetourt, a burgess, speaker of the House of Delegates, a judge, the first professor of law in an American college—at William and Mary—and a signer of the Declaration of Independence.

The study

The parlor

The dining room

The student's room

The furnishings of the Wythe House are predominantly of American origin. The high chest of drawers in the northeast bedroom *(above)* was made in Boston about 1740. The slant-top desk (about 1760) came from Rhode Island. In the southwest bedroom *(below)* all pieces are eighteenth-century American except the mahogany basin stand (English, about 1770).

Next page:
The spire of Bruton Parish Church overlooks Mr. Wythe's garden and stable yard.

WETHERBURN'S TAVERN

Henry Wetherburn owned or managed several of Williamsburg's most famous eighteenth-century taverns, sometimes more than one at a time. He was host at the Raleigh, for example, when he bought this property in 1738 and erected the eastern portion of the building. An inventory of his possessions, some of them doubtless acquired in his successive marriages to the widows of other innkeepers, has proved most helpful in refurnishing the tavern to its former state.

George Washington often dined or supped at Southall's, as the tavern was known in his day. Since most of the flooring is original, one may actually walk here in Washington's footsteps.

Mr. Wetherburn's inventory listed nineteen beds, indicating that he could put up for the night as many as thirty-eight persons, counting two per bed.

Every sort of food could be found in the tavern's busy kitchen.

From the paddock behind a small vegetable garden one sees the back of the smokehouse, the dairy, and a corner of the kitchen, with the wellhead and the rear of the tavern itself showing between them.

BRUSH-EVERARD HOUSE

John Brush, gunsmith, built the front portion of this simple home in 1717. It contains touches of elegance, however, such as the carvings that dress the central stairway. The most prominent of many later owners, Thomas Everard, served as clerk of York County from 1745 until his death in 1784. He was also auditor of Virginia and clerk of the General Court, and was elected mayor of Williamsburg in 1766. Appropriate to Everard's status and aspirations, a collection of books has been placed in the library; the titles are those listed by Thomas Jefferson in 1771 for the guidance of a young planter who wished to acquire culture as painlessly as possible.

The dining room

The northeast bedroom

The parlor

The library

Two views of the
southwest bedroom

The northwest bedroom

The gardener's
workshop
(opposite page)

RALEIGH TAVERN

This most famous of Williamsburg hostelries was dedicated to Sir Walter Raleigh, who took a leading part in sending colonists to the New World. His leaden bust adorns the main doorway. The Raleigh was a center for social and business activity and the scene of many public auctions of land, slaves, and goods. On at least two occasions members of the House of Burgesses met in rump session here to decide on policies and actions in opposition to those of king and Parliament.

Patrons of the public dining room could expect plain fare served, at regulated prices, on sturdy dishes of pewter and salt-glazed stoneware.

Besides keeping his own records, the innkeeper served as postmaster to both transients and townspeople. The ribbons tacked criss-cross to the wall held messages waiting to be claimed.

A blazing fire adds warmth and an air of hospitality to the taproom.

Players and onlookers both might bet heavily on the outcome of a game in the Raleigh's billiard room. The great table was made in England in 1738.

PEYTON RANDOLPH HOUSE

Like his father, Sir John Randolph, Peyton Randolph was a distinguished lawyer, an influential political leader, and speaker of the House of Burgesses. In that office from 1766 to 1775 and as president of the First Continental Congress in Philadelphia, he wielded enormous power in the struggle for American independence—generally on behalf of moderation. Comte de Rochambeau, commander of French forces in the siege of Yorktown, made his headquarters here while preparing for that battle.

The beautiful oak paneling of this bedroom is unique in Williamsburg.

The painted floor covering catches the eye
in Peyton Randolph's comfortable library,
while the mind recalls that his books, bought
from his estate by Thomas Jefferson,
became the nucleus of the Library of Congress.

The spacious center passage and
stairs *(opposite page)* were
characteristic of large colonial
Virginia homes.

The unique character
of colonial Virginia
architecture . . .

becomes evident
in the homes
and in the outbuildings.

Behind Waters Storehouse and the Printing Office

Ever so briefly, the city
feels winter's frosty touch.

The St. George Tucker House
(opposite page)

The Greenhow-Repiton
Brick Office

THE CRAFTS

An imposing array of elixirs and ointments, medicinal herbs, aromatic spices, and "Best Virginia" tobacco greets visitors to the Apothecary Shop. Most eighteenth-century apothecaries prescribed and dispensed medicines and fulfilled the role of surgeon as occasion demanded.

Opposite page: In the eighteenth century most gentlemen wore wigs and had them dressed regularly by the wigmaker. A lady's wig, or more likely her own hair, was dressed at home.

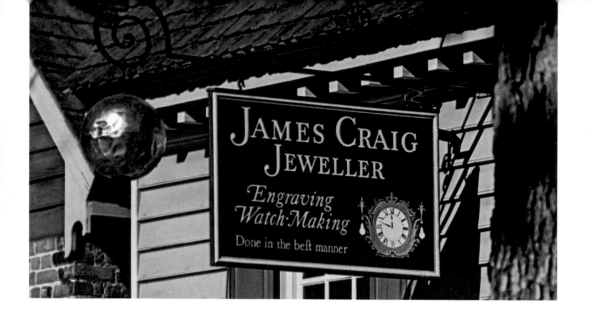

For those eighteenth-century colonists who could not read, the sign of the Golden Ball identified the shop where James Craig, master silversmith and jeweler, practiced his exacting trade.

"Minding his Ps and Qs" meant more to the colonial printer than just keeping his own counsel. It required a thorough knowledge of the type case, into whose many compartments his supply of hand-set type was sorted. At the Printing Office on Duke of Gloucester Street, the printer once more "pulls the devil's tail" of his ancient press to produce accurate examples of early printing.

In a small building to the rear, the bookbinder fashions elegant bindings, bookmarks, and notebooks. Here he draws a comb through a bath of colors to make the swirled pattern of marbled paper.

Horses were as common in Virginia then as automobiles are today. The saddler and harness-maker was an important man in the community.

Tidewater soil being sandy and free of stones, horses and oxen often went unshod. But every home and farm needed some items from the blacksmith's forge—axes, hoes, andirons, wagon tires, candle stands, and so on.

Like his predecessors since the first years at Jamestown, the gunsmith makes and repairs the locks, stocks, and barrels of all kinds of firearms.

Baskets woven of oak splits take many shapes and sizes. They are strong, light in weight, and long-lasting.

Opposite page:
The weaver at her loom in the Spinning
and Weaving House makes fine homespun
fabrics in the old ways.

Gingerbread men emerge from wooden
molds at the bakery of the Raleigh Tavern,
where the bakers turn out bread and cakes
using recipes, ingredients, and equipment
of colonial times.

A scarecrow keeps watch over the cornfield
before Robertson's Windmill, a post mill
of a type well known on the Virginia
peninsula in the eighteenth century.

Unlike their horses, eighteenth-century
citizens of tidewater Virginia were well shod.
The bootmaker fashioned his footwear by
hand on wooden lasts, with square, pointed,
or round toes as fashion dictated. But he
formed most shoes on straight lasts—without
distinction between right and left foot.
He also made leather dice cups, jewel boxes,
mugs, buckets, and other items to order.

"Black love ribands," "Sleeve Knots," "stuff Shoes for Ladies," "Cloaks and Cardinals"—such were the frills, finery, and necessities sold by Margaret Hunter and her sister Jane in their shop on Duke of Gloucester Street. Here once more are counters filled with soaps and buttons, fans, butterfly caps and mobcaps, knitting needles, breast flowers, and decorated hats of Tuscan and Leghorn straw.

The shinglemaker *(opposite page)*, flax-breaker, candle-dipper, and soapmaker depend on good weather to ply their crafts outdoors.

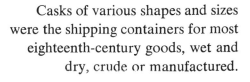

Casks of various shapes and sizes were the shipping containers for most eighteenth-century goods, wet and dry, crude or manufactured.

The musical instrument-maker *(right)* in his shop next to the cabinetmaker, the music teacher *(below)* in his place on Duke of Gloucester Street, and performers of many kinds testify that the sound of music is as important today as it was in colonial times.

In camp, in training, or in the field, fifers and drummers were essential to eighteenth-century army routine. They provided the everyday sounds of a soldier's life from reveille to tattoo, improved morale and discipline, and inspired the troops in combat. Colonial Williamsburg's fifes and drums provide music of the revolutionary period played by young musicians in authentic costume.

KING'S ARMS TAVERN

In the days of William Byrd III, King's Arms was one of the best-known taverns in the city of Williamsburg. During the Revolution its proprietress, Mrs. Jane Vobe, supplied food and drink to American troops, and Baron von Steuben, drillmaster of the Continental Army, was a regular patron. Today it specializes in traditional southern foods served in the hospitable atmosphere of another age.

Twentieth-century visitors may dine like their colonial forebears. Service is provided by "young Gentlemen of the College of William and Mary."

Today's bountiful fare of King's Arms Tavern.

CHOWNING'S TAVERN

An alehouse typical of the colonial period, Josiah Chowning's tavern served a less sophisticated clientele. In the tradition of that earlier day, Chowning's offers simple, hearty fare to its twentieth-century patrons.

In pleasant weather the airy, vine-shaded garden provides a place to pause for refreshment or enjoy a full meal.

The mellow warmth of Chowning's makes each
mealtime a memorable experience.

CHRISTIANA CAMPBELL'S TAVERN

Convenient to the Capitol and noted for good food, this popular house attracted many prominent leaders of the Virginia colony. George Washington and some of his friends had a club here.

Mrs. Campbell, the proprietress, was acknowledged to be a fine hostess. Later, however, a disgruntled would-be patron described her as "a little old woman, about four feet high; and equally thick, a little turn up Pug nose, a mouth screw'd up to one side."

Today Mrs. Campbell's tavern once more operates in the spirit of its eighteenth-century hostess.

COLONIAL WILLIAMSBURG

In 1926, inspired by the foresight and enthusiasm of Dr. W. A. R. Goodwin, then rector of Bruton Parish Church, Mr. John D. Rockefeller, Jr., became interested in the preservation and restoration of eighteenth-century Williamsburg, and thereafter devoted his personal attention and resources to the fulfillment of this goal.

The purpose of Colonial Williamsburg, in the words of the Board of Trustees, is "to re-create accurately the environment of the men and women of eighteenth-century Williamsburg and to bring about such an understanding of their lives and times that present and future generations may more vividly appreciate the contribution of these early Americans to the ideals and culture of our country."

Today, the Historic Area of Colonial Williamsburg embraces about 175 acres, the heart of the old city. There are eighty-eight original eighteenth-century and early nineteenth-century structures within and near this area. Several main buildings and many outbuildings that did not survive the years have been reconstructed on their original foundations after extensive archaeological investigation and historical research. Also, ninety acres of colorful gardens and greens have been re-created, using chiefly plants known to the eighteenth-century colonists.